1935 if you wanted to
read a good book, you needed
either a lot of money or a library card.
Cheap paperbacks were available, but their
poor production generally mirrored the quality
between the covers. One weekend that year,
Allen Lane, Managing Director of The Bodley Head,
having spent the weekend visiting Agatha Christie,
found himself on a platform at Exeter station trying to
find something to read for his journey back to London.
He was appalled by the quality of the material he had to
choose from. Everything that Allen Lane achieved from that
day until his death in 1970 was based on a passionate belief
in the existence of 'a vast reading public for *intelligent*
books at a low price'. The result of his momentous vision
was the birth not only of Penguin, but of the 'paperback
revolution'. Quality writing became available for the price of
a packet of cigarettes, literature became a mass medium
for the first time, a nation of book-borrowers became a
nation of book-buyers – and the very concept of book
publishing was changed for ever. Those founding
principles – of quality and value, with an overarching
belief in the fundamental importance of reading –
have guided everything the company has
done since 1935. Sir Allen Lane's
pioneering spirit is still very much alive
at Penguin in 2005. Here's to
the next 70 years!

MORE THAN A BUSINESS

'We decided it was time to end the almost customary half-hearted manner in which cheap editions were produced – as though the only people who could possibly want cheap editions must belong to a lower order of intelligence. We, however, believed in the existence in this country of a vast reading public for intelligent books at a low price, and staked everything on it'
Sir Allen Lane, 1902–1970

'The Penguin Books are splendid value for sixpence, so splendid that if other publishers had any sense they would combine against them and suppress them'
George Orwell

'More than a business … a national cultural asset'
Guardian

'When you look at the whole Penguin achievement you know that it constitutes, in action, one of the more democratic successes of our recent social history'
Richard Hoggart

Noise

HARI KUNZRU

PENGUIN BOOKS

PENGUIN BOOKS

Published by the Penguin Group
Penguin Books Ltd, 80 Strand, London WC2R ORL, England
Penguin Group (USA) Inc., 375 Hudson Street, New York, New York 10014, USA
Penguin Group (Canada), 10 Alcorn Avenue, Toronto, Ontario, Canada M4V 3B2
(a division of Pearson Penguin Canada Inc.)
Penguin Ireland, 25 St Stephen's Green, Dublin 2, Ireland
(a division of Penguin Books Ltd)
Penguin Group (Australia), 250 Camberwell Road, Camberwell, Victoria 3124,
Australia (a division of Pearson Australia Group Pty Ltd)
Penguin Books India Pvt Ltd, 11 Community Centre,
Panchsheel Park, New Delhi – 110 017, India
Penguin Group (NZ), cnr Airborne and Rosedale Roads, Albany,
Auckland 1310, New Zealand (a division of Pearson New Zealand Ltd)
Penguin Books (South Africa) (Pty) Ltd, 24 Sturdee Avenue,
Rosebank 2196, South Africa

Penguin Books Ltd, Registered Offices: 80 Strand, London WC2R ORL, England

www.penguin.com

First published as a Pocket Penguin 2005
1

The moral right of the author has been asserted

Set in 11/13pt Monotype Dante
Typeset by Palimpsest Book Production Limited,
Polmont, Stirlingshire
Printed in England by Clays Ltd, St Ives plc

Contents

Bodywork

Hi Ho

Sunday mornings I wash my car. The house is one of the new ones at the top of the hill, so while I run the shammy over the Sierra's shiny curves I can look over the allotments and see other earlybirds clearing and digging their little patches of dirt. I've never been much of a one for gardening. All that muck. If there's been a constant in my life it's that I've always liked to keep things neat. Of course, this is a nice area and it doesn't do to let standards slip, so after I've done the car I usually spray the front lawn, walking a little circuit with a canister of weedkiller on my back. Hi ho!

These Sunday mornings are my own. Cheryl never raises her head before ten-thirty, just refuses to. Sometimes she'll say she's 'a little indisposed'. I don't know about indisposed. Lazy, more like. The number of times I've brought her a cup of tea, trying to chivvy her up for some daytrip we've planned, and found her wrapped in the bedclothes looking up at the ceiling. Quite awake mind you. Just far away.

No daytrip today. I went out to the ringroad, to the Superstore.

A List

1. 15 metres rubber tubing (ultrafine) 2. 'Darco' (?) Bearings (x4) 3. 5x5m plastic laminate 4. Screws, bolts, washers, nuts etc. (various) 5. Aleph Industries 'Victor' pump (size 4) 6. Gold wire (20z wound) 7. 1 ltr SuperGrade lubricant 8. Fittings SA9858674a (x4), SA985867b (3), SD945536a (1), SX966632a, b, c (3 of each) 9. Roehmer-Sharpe dissection scalpel set (cat. A4765) 10. Sutures (RS cat. S3367) 11. Local anaesthetic 'Devorine' (25x5ml ampoules – Debronax or unbranded equivalent) 12. Sterile pads (RS cat. C35) 13. Tourniquet (or make one?) 14 SynaptoKit (get pro. Version – nb. important!) 15. Skin 2000 (4 sheets, caucasian) 16. Other (ask assistant).

Pretty Girl

Indeed she was, in her blue and white striped uniform. She helped me put the things in the boot. I smiled at her, hoping she would smile back. And she did. Looked like a photo I once saw in a magazine.

Favour

Afterwards I drove round to TD Repairs. I've a mate fixes things. Vacuum cleaners, tellies, radios, you name it. Barry, he said, take whatever you need. He showed me round the back, where he keeps the bits he's taken out. Left me to have a good old rummage around. I offered to pay him, but he wouldn't hear of it. Lovely bloke, Ted. I'd picked out quite a lot, circuit boards and so on. Still, he wouldn't take a penny.

Back Home

There are instructions to follow. It looks a little daunting, until you take the plunge. I lay all the stuff out on the table in the garage – I haven't got a proper workshop, one of the drawbacks of the house. And it's essential to keep things clean, especially with something like this, which is hard to do in the garage. Reluctantly I decide to keep the Sierra outside until I've got it finished. All that oil, not to mention the stuff it picks up on the wheels. When I go back inside for the bucket and mop I realize Cheryl's still not up. It's past twelve, which is unheard of even for her. Upstairs, all the curtains are drawn. I pop my head round the bedroom door.

'Are you ill, love? What's the matter?'

She doesn't answer. I notice there's a funny smell in the room, sort of sweet. I open the window, let a bit of air in.

'Well, what is it, love? It's almost lunchtime.'

'Go away,' she says. 'I'm fine.'

Step by Step

Choose a small square of tissue on the left forearm, just below the elbow. Make an incision on three sides (Fig. 1.13) taking care to cut no deeper than the layer of subcutaneous fat. Peel back and sprinkle with powder from the sachet provided. Taking your pre-cut square of laminate, affix it to the opened section, holding in place until it has fully adhered to the epidermis. Cover and leave. Repeat this over the whole forearm area until (Fig. 1.14) you have exposed the area shaded grey. You are now ready to isolate the flexor muscles, in preparation for the first series of implants.

Connections

receptor Eu.306.56	V CNS site 56 (red)
receptor Eu.306.57	V CNS site 56 (cyan)
receptor Eu.306.58	V CNS site 56 (magenta)
receptor Eu.306.59	V CNS site 56 (blue)
receptor Eu.307.00	V CNS site 57 (red)
receptor Eu.307.01	V CNS site 57 (cyan)
receptor Eu.307.02	V CNS site 58 (magenta)
receptor Eu.307.03	V CNS site 59 (red)
receptor Eu.307.04	V CNS site 59 (cyan)
receptor Eu.307.05	V CNS site 60 (blue only)

Mixed Feelings

Lately Cheryl's been watching a lot of that woman on the telly, the one who goes on about how people have needs. Not a good sign. We have our ups and downs, like anybody, and at the moment we're going through a low patch. It's hard to get much out of her. And she keeps giving me the same tea. We had boil in the bag cod in cheese sauce three times last week. I had to put my foot down. But in spite of minor niggles I have reason to feel quite pleased. I'm proud of myself, actually, and though she doesn't display much interest when I show her the blueprints, I think Cheryl will be too. It's a fiddly job, but I'm a match for it. Both the arms are finished. I can touch my face and feel the spongy fingerpads, my designer fingers touching my cheek. They smell of electrical showrooms, or the plastic covers on the upholstery of new cars.

Domestic Trouble?

No. Certainly not. If you think rattling a few pans counts as trouble, you should try watching that TV show. The things people will talk about in public! They ought to show more self-respect. Cheryl and I have what you might call a happy marriage. And she's certainly never gone without. It's our anniversary, as it happens. Twenty-three years today. We're going to a restaurant.

Le Pont d'Avignon

The waiter is decent enough. Often they'll hover round you, fluster you as you try to choose. Cheryl speaks some French, though as usual at the moment she isn't saying anything. When the wine comes she makes a grab for her glass, knocks it back and tells him to fill her up again. I'm extremely embarrassed. This is not the Cheryl I know. He says something funny to her with 'madame' on the end of it and she giggles like a bloody schoolgirl. Tosses back another glassful, and then belches. I decide I should say something.

'Pull yourself together, Cheryl. You're making a spectacle.'

'Shut up,' she says. She actually tells me to shut up, right there in the restaurant. And the waiter can hear too. Bastard starts sniggering to the girl who takes your coat.

'Cheryl!' Between my teeth, like. 'Why are you doing this?'

As I say it I notice how she smells. She was always a clean girl, Cheryl. I wouldn't have married her otherwise. At first I think it's a new perfume. It's sweet, but not pleasantly so. Rotten-sweet like something you've left out of the fridge too long. It's quite disgusting. And she's sweating. Her face is shiny and damp.

'Look, Cheryl. Love. It's obvious you're not well. We'd better be getting home.'

And she starts to laugh again.

'Not well, is it? Take a look at me, Barry. What is it you see?'

'Don't, Cheryl. You're playing games. You know I don't like it.'

'Come on *love*.' Just like that. Sneering. 'Come on *love*, answer me.'

'I don't know. You, Cheryl. I see you.'

'I don't think you see anything at all. But there's someone here, Barry. A human being.' And she begins to laugh.

I will never forget how she looks at this moment, her sweaty face split open by that horrible grin. Cheryl, *My Wife*, looks disgusting, dirty. I get up to leave, trying to pull my wallet out of my jacket. I just want to go. She never uses that sort of language normally. I tell myself she's ill, doesn't know what she's doing. But at the same time I realize there's a side to her I didn't know before, a crude side. And I'm afraid. I don't even notice if she's following me as I stuff a twenty pound note into the waiter's hand.

1.47 AM

Lingual sites are divided into four areas, roughly corresponding to the traditional distinctions between sweet, sour, bitter and salt (Fig. 32.4). To configure the unit, simply connect the input device to the temporary ports marked a through e. Key in the following strings to install default settings . . .

A Letter

Dear Cheryl. What is happening to us? I know that lately things have not been too good but tonight has made me worried about the future. I wish you would tell me what is happening and if I have done anything to you. It seems we are so far apart. We are both mature adult people Cheryl and we should talk it over. Lets get this thing straightened out.

Out. Out in the open. Let's put it on the table. Put our feelings . . .

It took me hours to work up to that. Hours just sitting in the garage with my head in my hard new hands. And now it doesn't seem quite right. I screw the paper up and throw it into the bin in the corner of the garage. I have to be careful not to make any big movements because I'm still hooked up to the little box.

a100Xon, a1200Xoff, a14400Xon, a144800Xoff, b100Xoff, b120Xoff, b2000Xon, b2200Xon, b11000(0), b12000(0), b12250(0), b14400Xon . . .

I'm staying put, right here in the garage. Been here all night, wasn't able to go to bed. I don't know what to do, because I can't stomach being in the same room with her.

She's my wife. I have a duty.

I was in the garden, some time after midnight, looking in through the kitchen window. There she was, in her nightie, drinking a glass of water. It was horrible. Everything, everything *underneath*, seemed to be rippling, moving about as if it were alive. I was horrified. What's become of her? What's going to become of us?

When I crept up to bed she must have been asleep. Waves of it, that rotten toilet smell, coming off her. Almost unbearable. The night light was still on, and she had one arm over the covers, the sleeve of her nightie all rucked up. The arm was all moist with sweat. It seemed to be pouring out of her in buckets. I tried to get closer to the bed and found my heart was racing, like I was going to have a seizure. I felt it was going to hammer its way out of my chest.

Pink. The droplets of sweat. On her arm. They were pink, like they were mixed with blood.

Fiddly Bits

There are parts which it is difficult to do yourself. I obviously couldn't ask Cheryl, so I gave Ted a ring. In a way I think he was quite flattered, and he came over as soon as you like. Having made the various preparations, some of which made me rather woozy, we pried open the chest cavity and got to work. I was glad of his help. He's nimble-fingered, old Ted, fitted the little sacs and tubes and whatnot onto the pump and before I'd really had time to draw breath (ha ha), we were having a swift half round the corner.

'Bit sore I expect, Barry?'

I must admit I didn't answer right off. I was far away. Preoccupied, to tell the truth. Something not quite right. I'd been looking forward to that pint, and now it tasted strange. Sort of metallic. I said as much to Ted.

'Why don't you send it back? Oi Derek! Derek?'

'Shut it, Ted!'

'I'm sorry?'

'Leave it alone, eh. Maybe there's nothing up with it. I'd rather you didn't.'

'Alright old son. No need to get all aggravated.'

I had to apologize to him after that. He took it well. Not one to hold a grudge, Ted. Promised to come back after work the next day and help me with the intestines.

Upstairs

I pulled back the covers. Cheryl is out, God knows where. I pulled back the covers and saw the brown stain her body had left from last night. I swear there are stains on her clothes too, and in the bath there's a mat of hair. Her clothes stink of rotten meat.

Holding my breath, I shoved some of them into a bin bag. Then I walked down to the bottom of the garden and burnt them.

Signs of Decay

I know Cheryl has been back, because there's a smell in the toilet. Since Ted and I had that stint last week I haven't actually needed to use it myself. I try to be in the garage whenever Cheryl's about, so I don't see her any more. I just find the signs. Shoes on the floor of the bedroom. Pans in the kitchen with food stuck to the bottom. It's coming into the hot weather. The flies are buzzing round. The place is a breeding ground for disease, but as I say, since last week, none of that digestive stuff is my concern.

Bit bothered to notice some scarring on the knees. In the manual it says the material's resistant, and I've hardly been doing anything too strenuous. God alone knows what would happen if I took it into my head to go rock-climbing, or play football. I was wondering about taking them back, getting a refund, but to be honest I can't be bothered. I suppose that's what they count on, that you can't be bothered. They're on, and they'll stay on.

Anticipation

When I get dirty I just take a cloth and wipe the surfaces down. Smooth, perfect. I can even shine them if I want to. A plastic skin, a barrier between me and all the muck and filth outside. Now there are only a few things left to do, but they're the hardest ones. You have to buy the module as a unit, comes from America. Though Cheryl doesn't know it, I've been saving up for some time. A little bit here. A little bit there. And now it's unpacked, little twists of polystyrene dotted about on the workbench. I'm excited. Look at the time, Ted'll be round any minute.

Section 275.12

Both UniSys™ anterior and posterior choroid plexus sets come ready configured for use with any US Standard CNS kit. Slots are available for all major intramedullar interfaces. If you find problems initializing the units please refer to the troubleshooting guide at the rear of this manual.

This is it.

The most important stage. After this everything will flow in straight lines. I'll always know what to do because the answers will be there inside. Neat rows of electrons stacked like soldiers on parade. Yes-no, yes-no, yes-no. I'm excited, and why not? The last fuzzy bit of me is about to fall away. I'll be as clean and bright and perfect as a racing car. All the dead stuff falling off me like leaves in Autumn.

Well, will you look at that? It's not often I get poetic. Never was one for it at school. The-boy-stood-on-the-burning-deck and so on. What could have brought it on now? The excitement, I expect. Will I still get excited, after? Will I still think of things like Autumn leaves?

This is it. After tonight I should know what to do with Cheryl, too. I saw her today, first time in weeks. Awful. She looked as if she's been smeared in her own – anyway, I couldn't bear to look at her. I can hear her now, upstairs in the bathroom. There's a damp patch spreading across the ceiling. Not to worry. The unit is sitting there on the table, ready to be popped in. Ted will be round in a minute, and after that it will all be plain sailing.

Deus Ex Machina

People say that everyone has a Guardian Angel. I don't object to that. It is *the way* they say it. The way they use it as a synonym for luck, or some other chance process. I find it demeaning to be reduced to a metaphor. The very phrase 'Guardian Angel' is an example of the worst kind of folk theology, but I'm not about to correct it here, since to do so to the satisfaction of a modern mortal audience would take several hefty tomes of scholastic argument. Even then, without favourable reviews and a large marketing budget it would not be read. Life is short and art is long, as some pagan put it, though he wasn't thinking of my kind of life when he said it.

I'm also not about to ruin my prose by placing 'Guardian Angel' in inverted commas every time it appears. Suffice it to say that terms such as deva, household god, tree-spirit, fetish and even pooka or leprechaun convey some aspect of what I'm doing here. I am immaterial, powerful, and quite hands-on in my approach. At one point we were all hopeful that some human would manage to complete the project of a Synthesis of All Religions, which would have explained all this without me having to bother. There were some diligent Germans, but the chance of success fell off some time ago. Even attempting it seems to have gone out of fashion since you lot finally invented computer games.

So, Guardian Angel it will have to be. Obviously you have questions. Yes, there is a God. Yes, He passeth all understanding and no, He absolutely did not make man in His image. That was a piece of Hebraic vanity which has caused untold mischief through the ages. Take it from me as one of the Heavenly Host, God is far weirder than even the fastest-whirling dervish or most strung-out stylite has ever imagined. Yes, we angels do dance on pinheads, and the usual number we fit on is one hundred and seventy-six for a standard gauge pin. This is not because of some restriction in size. As I say, we are entirely immaterial. It's just that for pinhead dancing, one-seven-six is the right number. Call it tradition.

On the question of organized religion, as far as we're concerned church is entirely optional. We say yes to rituals, penances, fasting, sacrifice – go ahead. But none of them are more effective than others. Sincerity is important. We appreciate that. But all these jihads and crusades, these isms and schisms, arguments over how many fingers to make the sign of the cross with, or whether to have images or smash them up, that's all way off the point. Basically, do what you like. Hang out. Take drugs. Sleep with each other. We want you to have fun, but for heaven's sake just try to be *nice*. You wouldn't think that was a lot to ask.

But all this is off the point. I am a Guardian Angel, and from the moment of her conception I have been looking after a young woman called Christina. Since the first proteins folded themselves into shape in the first cells of her embryo I have observed her with perfect, complete, angelic attention. As each filament of bone grew in her spine, each corpuscle of blood emerged in the miniature sac of her heart, I looked on, rapt and content, my Being fulfilled in the act of watching over her.

As is well known, God moves in mysterious ways. One of the most mysterious is His system of classification. To get technical for a moment, not everyone does have a Guardian Angel. Some people share. While not being entirely infinite, we angels do have extraordinary powers and capacities, so this is not such a bad deal for the sharers as first appears. Indeed there is a whole town in the Southern United States who only have one angel between them. This is not some kind of heavenly snub. They get excellent service. And there is a logical method to the assignment of angels. However it is the Deity's method, and manifesting His filing system is something God is particularly averse to doing.

So I look after Christina. Just Christina. I find my purpose in the vast, almost luminous love I bear for her, a love which is in its turn just a reflection of the implausibly humungous love which God bears for her, same as He bears for every living thing. Christina is twenty-eight years old. She has chestnut-brown curly hair that she wears long, in a kind of cloud which haloes her head as she walks. This causes other people to turn and watch her. She does not know this. Secretly she believes she is plain. This is partly because she has an unfashionable body, fuller and more womanly than is sanctioned by the style leaders of her particular place and period. But Christina is beautiful. Extraordinarily, achingly beautiful. The hollow of her navel, the line of her collar bone, the tiny pattern of whorls and grooves in her skin – I have observed all these come into being, and they are transcendent in their loveliness. She is sexy too. But then, I would say that.

Christina wants to be a poet. That is, she wants to be a published poet. She writes poems, has done since she was thirteen years old. They are very good, though that is not something she knows either. Christina doubts. She spends most of her day doubting, wracking herself with worry over her talent, her looks, her future prospects. Recently she has been wracking herself over her relationship with a man called Robert, who is worthless and has made her very unhappy. So unhappy, in fact, that Christina is wondering whether she wants to die. Right now she is in the bathroom of her friend's London flat, holding a bottle of tranquillizers, examining its label in front of the mirrored bathroom cabinet.

The bottle holds a great fascination for her. The smudged printing on the label helps her make a decision, reminding her as it does of school reports and council tax forms and other things she associates with impersonal, bureaucratic fate. To imagine her death Christina always thinks of it as abstract and inevitable, perhaps even as happening to someone else. So the formal printing confirms her suspicion that her time has come. In a few moments she will unscrew the bottle top, pour out a handful of pills, fumble with full palm and tooth-mug and tap, scattering pills like seed onto the hard porcelain basin, and finally swallow a gulp of tepid water and a gulp of bitter-tasting pills.

That's where I'll come in.

Christina looks at her face in the mirror. Her eye make-up has run and she thinks she looks like a panda, with her two dark circles and stained cheeks. Her image of pandas comes more from drawings in children's books than film or photos, and she has never seen one in real life, because the day her father took her to the zoo, the pandas didn't come out. In Christina's head, pandas always have the hint of a smile as they snack on a bamboo shoot, because that is the way the children's book illustrators drew them. Always a hint of human emotion. And so she smiles, to make herself look more like a panda, just for a moment in front of the bathroom mirror before she tries to commit suicide.

I know every inch of Christina's body and mind, each sensation, each mood. I know every one of her likes and dislikes, her favourite band, the place on her neck where she likes to be touched when a man is kissing her. I know the exact strength she likes her coffee and the words her grandmother whispered to her in the hospital just before she died. I also know the effect the handful of bitter pills will have on her physiology after she swallows them. I know every name of every chemical Christina will synthesize as each complex molecule of each pill starts to bond with receptors in her weary, stricken brain.

I certainly know far too much about Robert. Robert has a lot to answer for. At the book launch, he used a chat-up line on Christina which was old years before Boccaccio employed it in the *Decameron*. It is, in fact, a line which appears in variant forms in the literature of seventeen different cultures, including a version on a tenth-century runestone in Norway. And she bought it! Robert followed up his ancient chat-up line with a series of pushy, sleazy moves in a taxi and, over the course of several subsequent weeks, a further series of outrages which Christina told herself were passionate and exciting. In fact, during the nine months and seventeen days which ended yesterday, when Christina caught him booking a Caribbean holiday for himself and his other girlfriend, she thought Robert was amazing.

Robert was mainly amazing to Christina because he was a published poet who had won an award. Christina thinks Robert is witty, soulful, tormented and brave – in short, a genius. I think Robert is a cheap, pompous, arrogant fool, who stole most of his best lines from a Manchester poet he tutored on a Summer school ten years ago – a poet to whom, incidentally, Robert gave a 'B', telling him if he worked hard he might one day find something worth keeping. Robert is truly a sly, devious bastard. He is crap in bed too, though that is something Christina has been too lost in her fantasy of poetic love to notice, or at least to notice that she has noticed. I mean, it's not even as if he's good-looking.

I watch Christina swallow the pills. The face she makes is the same 'nasty taste' face she has made since she was four years old, a cascade of tiny tightening and relaxing muscles that is as familiar to me as the gesture she makes afterwards, a hand fluttering to her curly hair and brushing it with three fingertips. It was this gesture that made a young Frenchman called Hervé fall in love with her last year, in a café, in Paris. Christina had gone to Paris on her own, to pick up the pieces after a disastrous affair with a worthless-but-published man called Richard. She was sitting in the café nursing a *citron pressé* and trying to remember the lyrics to her-and-Richard's song, which she didn't know had also done time as Richard-and-Wanda's song, and Richard-and-Gaby's song. Trying to remember, her hand fluttered up to her hair.

Hervé was also a poet, and hence stood a good chance of gaining Christina's attention, though by nature he was shy and unpublished. Still he took his courage in both hands and tried to talk to the beautiful foreign woman. Unfortunately his English was poor, and Christina was too full of thoughts of

Richard to decipher what he was saying. She shooed him away, mistaking him for yet another of the legion of Parisian chancers who had tried to pick her up that afternoon. This was a shame, since she and Hervé would have been an inspirational couple. I have little doubt they could have shaped up as a Great Love. Instead Hervé dutifully pined away in his garret and Christina carried on floating around at poetry readings, ready to get picked up by creeps like Robert. Without the equanimity one gets from total prescience, knowing that sort of thing would make you sad.

Christina slumps down on the toilet seat, leans her head against the side of the basin, and shuts her eyes. Behind them, benzodiazepine molecules are nestling into her brain, shutting out all the worry and stress, chemical fingers smudging the delicate lattice of her thoughts, suggesting sleep, darkness, an ending. Against her cheek Christina can feel the contrasting sensations of cold porcelain and warm, fuzzy cloth, the collar of her favourite black sleeveless fleece. On the other side of the bathroom door, there is nobody. Just a living room with a coffee table on which sits a full ashtray, an empty bottle of vodka and a melted tub of ice cream. Paulette is out. Everybody is out. There is no one here in this flat with Christina, who came here to cry last night away on Paulette's sofa, under the spare duvet which smelt of other people.

As Christina loses her grip on consciousness and slumps to the floor, there is, just audible, the note of a well-tuned car engine in the street outside the flat. That is as it should be. Last night, as Christina worked her way through her bottle of supermarket vodka, exploring a chain of vodka-based memories which start with an unfortunate experience in a cinema car park aged sixteen, I was busy elsewhere, working behind the scenes to produce an alternative ending to the narrative my charge has created for herself. For the task, I have been using that greatest of labour-saving devices, the computer.

Computers are wonderful. Charles Babbage, Alan Turing, John von Neumann, even Bill Gates – all great favourites of mine. Since the marvellous machines penetrated every area of human society, my job has become considerably easier. You will of course find angels at work in all forms of technology, especially those which humans find complicated or hard to understand, like video recorders and fax machines. But the PC is the real centre of supernatural activity in the modern world. In an era when (due to trends in celestial politics it would be otiose to discuss here) miracles and overt manifestations of superhuman power have been banned under a strict convention, the scope for angelic intervention is severely limited. We do very little carrying aloft on shoulders, appearing bathed in golden light or other flashy stuff these days. That is a shame, but every true artist can turn restrictions to positive use. There is a certain beauty in minimalism, and my own preferred aesthetic is semiconductor-based.

In this case, to alter fate I have restricted myself to moving nothing larger than electrons. Specifically, I altered the charge of half a dozen selected spots on a tiny sliver of treated silicon in the Central Processor Unit of a PC which sits on the desk of an Estate Agent called Suzie. In this way I changed some ones into zeros, and some zeros into ones, halfway through the operation of a tricky date-calculation algorithm. My little nudge set off, domino-like, a cascade of instructions that made a single minor alteration to Suzie's diary software. This morning, she arrived in work to find that an appointment she remembered as being for mid-afternoon was in fact scheduled for early evening. She found she would have to stay late at work and show Mr Harakami the flat at seven tonight, or in other words, about five minutes from now. Paulette Conolly is keen to sell, and although the place is a little small, she thinks it might suit Mr Harakami's needs.

Naturally, I have performed a similar operation on Harakami's personal digital organizer, which really is a superb piece of engineering. So light, so compact! Now both agent and client believe they must have misremembered, and have made arrangements to meet three hours later than they expected.

The beauty of working with computers is their votive quality. As far as Estate Agents and Cartoonists (for this is Harakami Yukio's profession) are concerned, the dull grey boxes which take up such a prominent place in their lives might as well function by animal magnetism, or focusing cosmic rays. They are profound and mystical objects, things of whim and prophecy which require complete deference. Suzie and Yukio propitiate their machines, asking for fault-tolerance, viral absence and continued bug-free living and working. When dealing with the divine, human fallibility is thrown into sharp relief, so neither of the two has thought to question whether their computer has 'got it right'. They just obeyed. This is why angels find these machines so useful. They are the tools which replaced apparitions and holy relics.

Duly, Harakami Yukio and DeBrett Suzie are making small talk as they walk up the stairs towards an encounter with Christina's unconscious body, now picturesquely draped on the bathroom floor, the empty Diazepam bottle in the sink leaving no doubt as to the cause of her indisposition.

Paulette told Christina that she'd be back late because she was going out with Clive to talk things over. She told Christina that the Estate Agent was coming, and asked her to make sure the place was reasonably tidy. All this went in one grieving ear and out the other. Christina has spent her afternoon making a mess. There are sodden tissues, discarded sweaters, empty fag packets, the fall-out from several comfort snacks, and at least a dozen scribbled-on sheets of paper, relics of her attempt to tell Robert what she thought of him, in free verse.

Suzie's first thought, as she steps brightly into the living room and spies the detritus of Christina's day of depressed camping-out, is anger. Some people conspire to make her job particularly difficult. But there is no choice, she must tough it out, and so she smiles wanly at Yukio, who smiles wanly back. This is not because he is angry at the state of the flat. He is simply experiencing a sense of déjà vu. He has stood in this place before, breathing this very stale, smoky air with its undertone of something else, of a smell he wants to catch, to keep and savour. The smell of a person.

Just before Suzie steps trepidly over Christina's abandoned duvet and utters the fateful words 'and this is the bathroom', Yukio has an impulse to stop her, to give himself time to prepare for what is on the other side of the door. He will never understand why this is. But he finds he is not surprised to hear the sound of screaming. Yes, at the sight of Christina's body Suzie screams, a response conditioned by thousands of hours of televised police procedural drama. Bodies in bathrooms say 'crime scene' to Suzie, and by the time Yukio pokes his head round the door to find out what has upset her, she is already half-plunged into a nightmare of masked axemen and running down corridors.

Christina is looking good, which certainly wasn't her intention. She has fallen into a pose reminiscent of several major works of Japanese and European art. An Ophelia. A swooning Kunisada geisha. It also happens to be a pose in which Yukio sometimes draws his *manga* heroines, especially Lola Blue (of

Tokyo Blue Squad 2000), who often acts as the screen on which he projects his fantasies of ideal womanhood. This is all very convenient – not my doing at all I hasten to add, but nevertheless perfect. Of course, unlike Lola, Christina doesn't have eyes the size of dinnerplates or the figure of a pre-teen elf, but then Yukio is not very experienced with three-dimensional women.

So Yukio is struck first, not that there is a corpse in the bathroom, but that it is the corpse of a beautiful woman. Marvellous, if a little perverse, and very much in line with *manga* aesthetics. So much lies in that crucial first impression. By the time Suzie runs back into the living room, yelling extravagantly, Yukio has already inserted Christina's unconscious form into that mental list of 'things that make the heart quicken' which every human carries somewhere inside themselves. Most people's lists are unconscious, unexplicit, but every so often Yukio writes his down, in the manner of the tenth-century Japanese courtesan Sei Shonagon. 'The line of ink flowing from a fine-nib pen, the neon lights of the Ginza at night, a *Metal Gear Solid* high score, the beautiful dead girl with the cloud of chestnut hair . . .'

Yukio crouches, and deftly takes Christina's pulse. It is so slow and faint that his enquiring fingertips almost miss the tiny ebb and flow. But she is alive. The realization leaps in his chest like a bird.

'Call an ambulance,' he shouts to Suzie, unnecessarily. Still convinced that she has fallen into the plot of a slasher movie, Suzie is attacking the phone, calling everything from the police to an F-14 airstrike. Ten minutes away, a siren is already dopplering through the evening streets. Yukio experimentally slaps Christina's face a couple of times. She does not respond, and it makes him feel bad doing it, so he sits down next to her on the bathroom floor and pulls her head onto his lap.

This is how the ambulance crew find him. They take a look at the empty pill bottle, and inject Christina with a stimulant, which gets things going again, heartwise, but doesn't quite bring her back to consciousness. Yukio decides to accompany her to the hospital. He gets into the ambulance, and spends the journey staring at the girl's face, which, now it has a plastic airway stuffed into it, doesn't look as perfect as it did. Nevertheless Yukio is entranced, and every so often gives her limp hand a meaningful squeeze. Back in the flat Suzie is chain-smoking Christina's cigarettes, waiting for Paulette to come back from telling tedious, boring Clive that he is now tedious, boring and single.

What else is there to say? My work is done for the day and, in purely artistic terms, everything has gone swimmingly. There was a purity of form and intent which I find particularly moving. Satisfied with this as a statement, I can refrain from intervening again for some time. Once more I shall settle back to observe, my concentration absolute, my love for Christina undiminished. It will be interesting to see what happens. Yukio has his work cut out. *Manga* cartooning is not poetry. Japanese and English emotional registers are not always compatible. Christina is difficult, impetuous, far more articulate in her own language than he in his, and, these days at least, pretty screwed-up. But stranger couples have been made, some of them by me, and, like Hervé, Yukio improves with acquaintance. I hope he realizes he is a lucky man. He is being given an opportunity. His face will be the first thing Christina sees when she wakes up. To her, it will look like the face of an angel.

Memories of the Decadence

At the beginning of the Decadence things were easy. Although we were bored, and though everything had been done before, we were seized with a peculiar sense of potential. Our anomie had something optimistic to it. It was the golden age of our decline.

During the Decadence we went for promenades in the poorer quarters of the city, pausing to examine choice deformities, examples of disease or dementia. Soon we began to imitate them, at first only in mannerisms, later using make-up, drugs, prosthetics, or surgery. At length it became impossible to tell the fashionable from the afflicted. We thought this a salutary moral lesson, and took great delight in ignoring it.

During the Decadence we ate and drank to excess, until a point came when excess went out of fashion. Then we would revert to an extreme frugality. Mathematicians told us the attractor governing our consumption was a simple period which, though occasionally disrupted by shifts elsewhere in the libidinal economy, was reasonably easy to map. Manufacturers of luxury foods and the proprietors of health farms, spas and colonic irrigation parlours learned to track the so-called 'Bulimia Cycle', and for a time such businesses became extremely profitable. Soon however, activity became so intense that the pattern was disrupted and our predictions went awry, setting in motion a wave of bankruptcies, suicides and social ostracisms.

During the Decadence we gave up sexual intercourse, substituting for it various kinds of fetishism. We refined our tastes, narrowing their range and fantastically increasing their complexity. Certain people became interested in abstraction, concentrating perhaps on household objects or patterns of light and shade. Such citizens were known to climax spontaneously at the sight of a safety pin or a line of red tail lights stretching forward along a dual carriageway. One celebrated roué took his pleasure entirely from the contemplation of lipstick stains on the rims of Waterford crystal champagne flutes. He claimed this stemmed more from an appreciation of colour and texture than any displacement of the presence of a woman onto the glass.

During the erotic phase of the Decadence, combinations of time, place, mood and the presence of physical objects became ever more specific. An increasing percentage of resources were dedicated to sexual research and organization. Orgasms began to require corporate sponsorship, a trend which reached its apogee in the meticulously-planned bacchanals at Nuremberg, Shanghai and Hyde Park. The latter, in which an estimated two hundred thousand people participated in a ritual designed solely to produce the little death in a middle-aged software billionaire, was considered the highpoint of the movement. A cluster of massively-parallel processors was connected to a variety of front-end delivery devices. When triggered they instantiated patented pleasure-algorithms in the crowd, causing runaway positive feedback which was gathered into a series of giant cells, amusingly styled to represent luminous *linga* and *yoni*. When the charge had accumulated to a sufficient degree it was fed back via a fibre-optic core to the Park Lane hotel suite where the entrepreneur lay, bathed in the glow of his hi-res monitors. The crowd themselves, devotees of the influential cult of auto-erotic consumption, financed the event through ticket sales and the purchase of various items of merchandising. The energy generated by their activity produced a small quantity of almost-clear seminal fluid on the raw silk sheets of the billionaire's bed, and augmented his bank balance by an estimated twelve and a half million pounds. It was thus considered a success and plans for a two-hundred date world tour were drawn up, only to be scotched by his premature death from skin cancer in a Hawaii tanning dome. Soon afterwards, a fashion for feverish masturbatory interiority gained favour, inaugurating a rage for Keats, broom closets and antique printed pornography. Boarding schools were set up throughout the country. The days of the megabacchanals drew temporarily to a close.

The involvement of large numbers of people in

organized sexual experimentation necessitated the development of information networks, directories and algebraic search engines dedicated to matching those of compatible tastes. Nymphets were put in touch with elderly professors, cyborg freaks with the manufacturers of Japanese industrial robots, those interested in coercion with those who wanted to be coerced. This last category caused some problems among purist dominants, for whom the desire to be coerced disqualified some candidates from consideration as slaves, concentration camp inmates or members of religious orders. A standard disclaimer form was quickly developed. Willingness to sign meant automatic barring as an involuntary submissive.

During the Decadence, eroticism itself was only a passing fad. The information network which grew up to enable efficient sexual contact became itself the object of our interests. Connoisseurs of classifications, indices and filing systems paid astronomical sums for rare databases. We became collectors of objects, not from any particular interest in the things themselves, but simply for the opportunities they presented us for cataloguing. Some citizens rejected computer automation altogether, taking great pride in feats of card-indexing. Cross-referencing by hand became an art as much appreciated as sculpture or the programming of combat games.

We soon developed an acute awareness of taxonomy. Classification according to phylum, genus and species became *de rigueur*, not just for biological material, but in many other fields as well. Televised public debates were held over the correct designation of common phenomena. They were conducted along the lines of mediaeval theological disputations, and took place in a studio mocked up to represent the cloisters of the twelfth-century University of Bologna. The only anachronism was the pair of bikini-clad girls who operated the digital scoreboard.

We engaged in a passionate love affair with hierarchies, all the more intense for our awareness that they were meaningless, even ridiculous, as tools for understanding our distributed, networked world. As the ebbs and flows of our frenzied culture became more extreme, we turned to the verities of dead, static systems of comfort ourselves, soothing the ache of the data pumping ever faster through our red-raw flesh. We relearned Abulafia's Caballah and studied the circular taxonomies of the Catalan, Ramón Lull. We rejected Watson and Crick for Paracelsus and John Dee, embraced Galen and the four humours, studied the Tree of Knowledge, the Body Politic, the Great Chain of Being and the angelology of the Scholastics. We wept at the beauty of the Metaphysical Grammarians, and yearned to know the true Hebrew God spoke to Adam before the flood.

Eventually the cult of learning collapsed altogether and, with it, the preoccupation with self-definition which had driven the entire early period of the Decadence. Citizens no longer cared to record or understand the minutiae of their personal experience.

They left themselves unexplored. After the collapse of all extant systems of knowledge, a feature of the early decadent period, subjective experience had become the only reference point for establishing meaning or value. Ceasing even to ask what one wanted thus became considered the most advanced form of transgression. Embracing this, we conducted the pursuit of pleasure in a lacklustre, half-hearted way. If we stumbled on something we liked, it was purely by chance. Maybe we would return to it. More often than not we would limp off somewhere else. There were many casualties. Service industries suffered dreadfully. Aesthetics collapsed as a discipline.

During this critical period of the Decadence, we did whatever we could to avoid the act of choice. We chose our political leaders via a lottery, and organized our social lives by an ingenious system of random number generation. Many citizens abandoned even their most basic body functions to chance. Gambling disappeared as a pastime, since none of us were interested in beating the odds.

Pure randomness soon fell into decline. Some definition returned, though our codes were still fuzzy, unclear and imprecise. The *vague vogue*, as it became known, lasted some time, though the inexact measuring systems in use during this phase render impossible any accurate statement of its length, impact, or intensity. It was a time of rumour, myth, superstition and nameless fear. Certain revisionist scholars have accordingly refused to recognize it as a historical entity, since it seems in so many ways continuous with the rest of our troubled, fluid times.

Having exhausted the most arcane possibilities of body and mind, having become bored with boredom itself, we began to adopt postures of total commitment. Ideologies were formed, wars fought, and causes died for, all in a spirit of absolute hedonism. We believed because it pleased us to believe. Our crusades and jihads were as bloody as any in history. We performed breathtaking acts of self-sacrifice and exacted violent retribution on our enemies. Bizarre monotheisms arose, whose fiery ill-worded theologies afforded ample opportunity for schisms, heresies and apostasy. There were public crucifixions. Young men with faraway eyes held their hands in flame rather than sign documents of recantation. Soon totalitarianism swept through our cities, bringing tanks and napalm in its wake. We covered the earth in ashes. The devastation ushered in a period of mourning, during which we wept rivers of tears, planted trees and erected monuments whose poignancy matched the vastness of our remorse. Joy followed hard on the heels of our mourning. Lassitude followed joy. Our prophets and scientists ran simulations to predict the next lurch of our communal whims, but each time their code was outdated as soon as it was compiled. The cycle ran faster, cults and movements swarming like flies on a carcass, paradigms blooming and withering like exotic cancers. Soon there was only speed, a sensation of pure intensity.

Then one day the Decadence ended. We began to be moderate in all things. Our decisions were considered, the product of sound judgement. Our institutions stabilized and prepared themselves for steady growth. We quoted maxims to each other: 'A little and often'; *'Mens sana in corpore sano'*. Now our economists have quelled the speculators, advocating cooperation and a sound industrial base. We believe in the family, in community and an undefined spirituality, aimed primarily at the regulation of sexual conduct. Debating is of no interest any more. We want a quiet life. 'All to the good', as we often say to our neighbours. We are content. And yet . . . And yet there is something stale in the air. Citizens whisper in the social clubs. They say that it cannot last.

Eclipse Chasing

Although we manufacture the ECLIPSE system, we don't make any decisions in regard to its use. That's a matter for the politicians. It's an important distinction, but a terribly hard one to get across. Our position as a company is clear: we feel it's basic good citizenship to do what we do, which is to provide government with the technology it requires to keep people safe. We cherish safety and are frankly surprised anyone would argue against it. Don't these people have children?

Vernon is trying to make this point to a group of protestors from the camp outside the gates.

'This is not a military facility,' he is saying. The protestors are dressed as negated corpses, which I think is rather tasteless. Two butch-looking women have chained themselves to the perimeter fence. The others are chanting slogans and trying to unfurl one of their zero-design-sensibility banners. I think Vernon is acquitting himself well. He has a very masculine presence. And a beautiful voice. Most people would be grateful to have a conversation with such a well turned-out young man.

'We are a private company,' says Vernon, summoning his most serious expression. 'We provide the nation with vital equipment as well as fun products for everyday use. Great banner, by the way.'

Now I think he's beginning to flounder. Complimenting them never works. One of the things which gets to me about the protestors is that they have no concept of excellence. It's like, unless some deprived Canadian kid can have it, you can't either. I think that's awful. The shouting increases in volume. There is audible profanity. It looks as if it's time to call in an OBV.

I go to the bike and phone Broadcast, who say they'll scramble one right away. It's a good thing, because while I'm gone a COMPRO takes place. COMPRO is a Customer Response acronym for 'comestible projectile'. They're a depressingly frequent occurrence. I return to find Vernon raising his voice, which is contrary to best practice. He has egg yolk all down his dove-grey tunic and is quoting statistics to the protestors about food waste, animal welfare and early-year nutritional deficits in zones of conflict. I wouldn't have bothered, myself. Demonstrating these people's hypocrisy may be intellectually satisfying, but it rarely brings results.

Overhead I can hear the rotors of the Outside Broadcast Vehicle. Vernon withdraws from the fence and we take cover behind the bikes, sealing our helmets before it touches down. Some of the protestors know what's coming and make a run for it. Others choose not to move. The two chained to the fence are, of course, immobilized. The broadcast is quite low-level, but you can tell it has an impact. They roll around, retching and spasming. One appears to have passed out.

When it's over we distribute the usual disclaimer notices, reminding the protestors of our legal right to use a broadcast system, our previously-established indemnity against claims for physical or psychological ill-effects, and so on. If they aren't fully conscious we just tuck it into their dungarees. To show there's no hard feelings, the pack also includes vouchers, a fragrance tester and a cartridge featuring some of the great new signings to our entertainment division.

The problem we face is that however many times we tell them we're not political, the protestors don't believe us. They insist against all logic that because we developed ECLIPSE, we hold some responsibility for Calgary and Thunder Bay. It's a point of view which has caused real downward movement on our stock price, and behind the scenes our lobbyists are pressing government for some kind of tax credit. We have carried the can for ECLIPSE despite substantial interests in the youth sector, where an association with eclipsed cityscapes negatively impacts volume. That ought to count for something.

The altercation with the protestors has made us late. It's time we got back to the Hub to participate in this afternoon's Opportunity. I capture a few stills for the log (mostly dazed protestors holding their information packs), while Vernon dabs at his egg-stain with a pre-moistened wipe.

'Vernon dear, you didn't win many hearts and minds in that engagement,' I tease.

'Pat-*ric*-ia,' he drawls, 'just button it, why don't you?'

I hate it when he calls me Patricia, especially on duty. It's so unprofessional. When I tell him this, he points out that addressing your co-workers as 'dear' or 'miss thing' is also unprofessional. We rev up the bikes and sulk all the way back to the Hub.

Though we bicker, Vernon and I are a great team. Customer Response is a relatively new field – and a challenging one. Candidates with a security background often lack presentational style, and people who have worked in old-fashioned corporate communication are accustomed to producing promos or setting up interviews, rather than face-to-face crowd work. For me it's a perfect combination. I've always been into the gym, and the chance to combine my excellent interpersonal skills with the application of non-lethal force is just fantastic. Vernon feels much the same. He used to be a diving champion. Under that tunic he still has a great body.

In a high-stakes context like ECLIPSE, there is an armoury of PR tools we can bring to bear. One night last month our landscaping team surrounded the camp at the main gate and working in complete silence and darkness planted thousands of daffodils and dwarf pear trees. The logistical challenges were considerable, but it went off without a hitch. The protestors reacted exactly as we expected. When they woke up and found themselves enclosed on all sides by attractive flora, they conducted a non-hierarchical decision-making process (something which always takes them ages) and decided the company gardeners must have had some sinister purpose. So they emerged from their yurts and uprooted everything. We recorded the event from a hide, and were able to distribute dramatic images of angry hippies trashing trees and flowers. No one likes to see that kind of thing. Several of their queasier backers withdrew support.

We roar up to the Hub and push the bikes back onto their kickstands. It's busy. As ever (when we have an audience) we make a big performance of taking off our gloves and unzipping the body-armour plates from our uniforms. Then we walk fabulously through the crowd, carrying our helmets like astronauts and drawing admiring glances from the news crews. In the vestibule, junior employees are distributing electronic press kits to reporters wearing the latest hair and teeth, who are taking turns recording pieces to camera in front of the water feature. This afternoon's Opportunity is particularly busy because a senior government minister is arriving to tour the new Ethics Park.

The park project was initiated by Terry, our visionary CEO. The government is keen to highlight the contrast between us and the Canadians, who have no tradition of human rights and follow a cruel and judgemental religion. So ethics are hot and Terry sees the park as a way to position us to bid for postwar cultural contracts. We are going to help rebuild Canada, says Terry. We are going to put in place the edutainment infrastructure they so desperately need.

On the dot of three, the minister arrives in a domestically-manufactured car, flanked by synchronized outriders. She steps onto the red carpet, is greeted by Terry (who dashingly kisses her on both cheeks), waves to the cameras and drops her coat to reveal a stunning lavender evening-gown, slashed at the thigh. Then she signs autographs for some competition winners and is ushered into the park.

Vernon and I are on security detail. We walk either side of the main crowd of dignitaries, maintaining constant contact with Broadcast through our earpieces. I love VIP detail. It's that feeling of being part of something, in this case a tightly-controlled network of people, computers and weaponry. This afternoon Terry has assembled a fantastic tour party, showcasing our best studio and management talent. The minister is meeting turbo-folk stars Jantalia and Ercole, several cast members from *Whose Surgery?*, our head of engineering and a decorated war hero who single-handedly wiped out a platoon of Canadian special forces at the battle of Salmon Arm. I would have left out the war hero. During the action he received eighty-percent burns, and most of his major body functions are assisted by devices in his chair. But Terry has a sure touch, and what the war hero lacks in aesthetics, he makes up for in ethics. Ethically, the war hero is unbeatable.

The minister makes conversation, asking Terry about the company's new products and dropping the name of a mutual friend. She tells the war hero he is heroic and asks Ercole about his forthcoming tour. She has been beautifully briefed. As an ethnically-diverse ensemble plays a panpipe arrangement of 'Do Right Woman', Terry leads the way through the entrance to the viewing platform, where the party contemplates a vista landscaped to represent the stern but simple world of the ancient Greeks. The park is contained in a climate-controlled dome, which rotates through a complete day and night cycle every thirty minutes. At the centre is the Arch of Decency, which (as Terry tells the minister) stands twenty metres high and is ingeniously formed from a pair of giant naturalistic hands, both holding symbolic objects. The giant hand on the left is clutching the sword of righteous justice, while the giant hand on the right has the trusty shield of fair play. Terry hits a prearranged mark and reels off his speech about the Arch, allowing the official photographer to take a picture of him pointing towards it, backed by the company logo. Terry points out that the hands cast a shadow over the park, which moves position every seven and a half minutes, pointing to each of the cardinal points of the compass in turn. He describes the park's twenty-one zones, each devoted to an important ethical principle: transparency, voluntary consent, full disclosure, equality of opportunity, avoidance of unnecessary mental suffering and so forth. Each zone incorporates a number of attractions and a pavilion where visitors will be able to purchase themed gifts and refreshments.

'I really have to congratulate you,' says the minister to Terry. 'It's so – *coherent.*'

Terry nods sagely. 'We did a lot of modelling,' he tells her. 'This disposition of resources sat at a notable peak in the fitness landscape.'

One of the actors interrupts to ask the minister about her jewellery. They have been told only to speak when spoken to and Terry looks annoyed. The actor realizes his mistake and tries to fade away, but it's too late: Terry's PA is already making a note. Unobtrusively I position myself beside them, so as to be able to intervene if there is anything unseemly in the way of pleading or remonstration. Luckily the actor just pales and stutters something about needing the rest room. I have one of the park staff escort him back to the Hub, just in case.

The park is a showcase for us, because it has been made and project-managed completely in-house. From structural engineering through to graphic design, the entire hundred-acre site is our work. This is why it's such a calling card. It's common knowledge around the Hub that the project isn't intended to break even. Though we are rumoured to be expect-

ing a huge loss, Terry supposedly foresees an upside
of seven figures, because with the park the minister
will be unable to deny us the Canadian contracts.

It's almost a done deal.

We walk through the Right to Life zone, where
the minister is especially taken by the interactive
termination. We all have a great time hitting the little
pop-up heads with the rubber mallets. It's going
fantastically. Every so often the sky in the dome dark-
ens, thunder rolls, and a giant holographic prophet
(played by one or other of our major studio stars)
appears and intones a snappy tenet from one of the
major world religions. THOU SHALT NOT KILL!
growls Jonty Ving, sporting a wonderful beard. ONLY
EAT FISH WHICH HAVE FINS AND SCALES
DETACHABLE FROM THE SKIN! warns Catherine
Colostomo, who makes the best of the material but
must be looking for a better agent. The minister is
enchanted.

The trouble comes when we are on the Freedom
Train, a dark ride which forms part of the Cultural
Sensitivity zone. At first everything seems normal.
We board small open carriages, held snugly in our
seats by foam-covered restraining bars. Animatronic
figures and video projections tell the story of freedom from the first moment of moral decision
through to today's culture of global liberty. We are
in a section explaining the importance of govern-
mental protection when I notice that one of the
animatronic terrorists is dressed differently from the

45

others. Over his lumberjack shirt someone has tied a white bib with the slogan **ECLIPSE IS EVIL** written on the front. Before I have time to respond the train moves on, whirring along the track towards the next tableau.

I try to raise Broadcast but can't get a signal. This makes me nervous. It's possible the ride's controls are interfering with my headset, or perhaps the steel skeleton of the tunnel is acting as a Faraday cage. Either way I don't like it. I'm no longer part of a network. I can't even confer with Vernon, who is sitting in the rear carriage. I am at the front, several seats ahead of the minister. It's too dark to see her expression, so it is impossible to tell if she's noticed the security breach. Perhaps the shirt is an isolated incident, one of the technical or maintenance staff making a statement. If that's the case it will be simple enough to fix. I hope so.

When the train comes to a sudden halt I realize the situation may be more serious. We have stopped beside a large plasma backdrop, which is supposed to accompany a tableau portraying the origin of the freedom to choose. Yesterday, at the technical rehearsal, avuncular figures dressed in period clothing, representing the founders of Safeway, Tesco, Piggly-Wiggly and Fnac sang a song about consumer empowerment while the screen relayed a montage of quaint historical adverts. Now the figures have gone and the screen is an ominous uniform blue. Several of the tour party realize something is amiss, and begin to squirm in their seats. I try to raise the restraining bar, but find it is clamped down tight. With some difficulty it is possible to twist round, but getting out is impossible. I am trapped! The minister is trapped! *Terry* is trapped! I can feel panic rising up in my chest, but my training kicks in and I force myself to visualize a pyramid located at the innermost centre of my being. Controlling my breathing I place the panic inside it, where it can do no harm. Then I reach down to my belt and unholster my weapon.

Voices murmur in the darkness. The tour party is increasingly uneasy. Terry tries to turn the situation round, joking loudly about whether he really did remember to pay the electricity bill. There are a few muted titters. His PA is frantically hissing into her headset. She also seems to be having communications problems.

'Vernon?' I call out. 'Everything OK back there?'

'All fine,' he responds.

I am about to suggest we try to force the bars when the screen flickers into life. The monochrome blue field is replaced by pixellated grey-black, then by a series of weird lurching images. The first thing I am able to make out is a date-stamp in the corner. Four months ago. What happened then? The footage is soundless, below broadcast quality. Someone pans a camera across the ground, jolting it, briefly levelling, then pointing it back at their feet. We're being forced to watch something unedited, something which absolutely should not be there on this screen in this place. I struggle against the restraining bar but it will not give. It seems to be clamping me even tighter than before, though perhaps that's the panic seeping out of its pyramid. The screen shows a pile of building waste, a fallen wall. Perhaps it's a construction site. The camera jolts around and settles on a sort of twisted black stalk, standing on the rubble like a giant liquorice twist.

Then I see what it is. The other people on the tour see too. There is an audible groan. The camera is remorseless, zooming in close, forcing us to watch the disgusting sight. I can't tell if it's a woman or a man, but it's still alive, more or less. Its face is a single open sore. What skin it has left is hanging off its body in charred flaps. It takes a faltering step towards us. At the back of the train someone begins to whimper.

Mercifully the camera jolts again, shakily panning across a landscape that I realize was once a street. Half-melted tangles of reinforcing rods poke up over the rubble. Corpses are everywhere, black streaks scattered over the whiteness like burnt matches. Behind me Terry is shouting for security. His voice is oddly broken and high-pitched. I find this upsetting in itself. Terry usually has such a mellow tone. 'Switch it off!' he squeaks. 'Switch it off right now!'

I am numb. This is just terrible. The screen flickers and reappears in what must have been an office. A computer keyboard sits incongruously in a pool of liquidized something-or-other. I don't want to know what. I want to close my eyes. Attached to the keyboard, the fingers welded onto the keys, is a hand. The camera executes a jerky zoom. The hand is wearing a wedding ring. I can hear someone throwing up into the foot-well of the carriage behind me. I think it's the minister.

Then we are back on the street. Survivors are stumbling around, horribly wounded. A woman carries something small and hideous in a blanket. A little girl cries for her missing hair and teeth. I know where this is now. The news channels showed a few images of Calgary, but they were mostly aerial shots, accompanied by stirring commentary about our victory. But this is the same city. These are the effects of ECLIPSE.

Then, as suddenly as it started, the tape stops and the screen reverts to blue. The restraining bars spring up, releasing us from our seats. There is a moment of silence, then everyone begins talking at once. People are hysterical, scared. Most of the actors and singers are in tears. I am outraged, angry in a way I've never been before. I never realized. It's appalling. Who is responsible? Who could do this? What kind of degraded individual could put us through such a disgusting experience? Turning around, I see the tour party's worried faces, bathed in blue light. I call out to see if Terry and the minister have been hurt. Then Vernon and I take our weapons and go to search for the perpetrators.

Finally I understand the kind of people we're dealing with. So far we've given them an easy ride, but it's time to stop pussy-footing around.

Godmachine™ v.1.0.4

TheoSystems Software Inc. Berkeley CA

This Read Me is divided into the following sections

- What is Godmachine™?
- New Information and known incompatibilities
- Installation and configuration
- Bifurcation warning [**important**]
- Support and Contacts

- *What is Godmachine™?*

Godmachine™ is a standalone cosmic creation utility, designed to allow the user to bring into being a universe with coherent ontology and physical laws. It can be run both in 'free will' mode, which allows the user to intervene actively in all stages of the cycle of birth and death, or in 'emergent' mode, which will instantiate a world-mind or supreme consciousness in the universe in parallel to the material creation. If total negation of all that exists in the user's own continuum is not desirable, please stick to running in 'free will' mode.

• *New information and known incompatibilities*

Godmachine™ 1.0.4 is known to be incompatible with almost all other executive command configurations, and may cause your belief system to crash if you attempt to run them at the same time. Don't say we didn't warn you!

Godmachine™ 1.0.4 is not currently compatible with AutoDrive Spacetime Continuum, Augustine Systems Transwarp Accelerator 2, Big Beaver Software's World Wobbler or any other ontological initiation utilities that do not support Apple virtual memory.

Some hardware add-ons, especially early versions of the Advanced Paradigm Koan accelerator card or Babylon MMTU drives are not compatible with Godmachine™ 1.0.4. The first version of Sand Data's Dreamtime Resolver card assigns paradigms in a way which conflicts with certain of Godmachine's creation routines. We advise upgrading hardware to at least Resolver II before attempting to run Godmachine™.

• *Installation and configuration*

[Fig. 1.0] Executive Circuit One [Governor]:

10.   LET GOD = LOVE

20.   LET LOVE = [LOVE] + 1

30.   IF [LOVE] • • THEN GOTO 50

40.   GOTO 20

50.   RUN GOD.EXE, COSMO$string, LET VOID =
      dim[0,0,0], LET VOID = [dim+1:FORALL/
      EXNIHILO], RUN 7DAYS.EXE

60.   [LOVE] PRONOUNCE$string SAYS
      [NAME]"[PROPHET,] ANDOR
      [WORLD_TEACHER]", = [SACRED WORD]
      AUM$string

70.   LET AUM$tring = [LOVE], LET
      PRONOUNCE$tring/[NAME] = [PROPHET]

80.   ROOT [CLOCK 0,0], AUM$tring = [WORD],
      LET [WORD] = GOD. ROOT GOD [RUN
      CLOCK]

90.   RUN MIRACULAT.EXE, OMNIPO.EXE,
      OMNIPR.EXE

100. GOTO 10

Godmachine™ 1.0.4 is unusual in that the key
executable codestring must be entered manually. This
is a safety procedure, designed to avoid accidental
cosmological initiations. Should Godmachine™ be run
using parameters other than those recommended in
the manual supplied, TheoSystems Software Inc.
cannot be held responsible. Likewise, TheoSystems
Software Inc. accept no liability for annihilations,

voidings, devastations or other cosmic wrath events occurring through misuse of Godmachine™.

The above code [Fig. 1.0] specifies a *primal* governing loop. No other codestring should be assigned equal priority. Above all, please check all applications running in parallel with Godmachine™ 1.0.4, and assign competing governors **lower priorities**.

Positive feedback generated by the governing circuit is used to drive the logochip, the Miraculator™, and a number of the vision functions. If you are not using the default bible, please refer to the manual to see how you should configure your sacred text to run most efficiently with the onboard logochip. NB: TheoSystems cannot offer support on nonstandard logochipsets.

• *Bifurcation warning*

Warning! Simulations have shown that a bifurcation is likely when variables a through d in codestring [alpha, omega] reach thresholds of 1.765, 3265.562, 4.001 and 1.000, respectively. It is unfortunately extremely difficult to predict which shift combinations may produce these values. As a general rule it has been found best to avoid polytheistic startups with heterodoxy settings greater than 5.652. If Godmachine™ 1.0.4 generates a high order pandimensional worldmind and proceeds to colonize unassigned areas of phase space, there is nothing for it but to reboot your machine. Do this **quickly**, as delay may result in user reconfigurations or even (rarely) user annexation to one or more Godmachine 1.0.4 routines. TheoSystems Software Inc will not be held responsible in such an eventuality. Users run Godmachine™ at their own risk.

* *Support and Contacts*

This product is shareware. If you like Godmachine 1.0.4, support the shareware concept and send $10 to TheoSystems, 1325 Banyantree Drive, Berkeley CA 94702, USA. Happy creating!

POCKET PENGUINS

POCKET PENGUINS